Daphne's Lot

Also by Chris Abani:

NOVELS

Masters of the Board
Sirocco

POETRY

Kalakuta Republic

Daphne's Lot

CHRIS ABANI

RED HEN PRESS   LOS ANGELES

Book & Cover Design: Mark E. Cull

ISBN 1-888996-62-5
Library of Congress Catalog Card Number: 2002110156

Publication of this volume is made possible in part through support by
the California Arts Council.

Red Hen Press
www.redhen.org

Third printing

First Edition

For

Daphne

Whose dreams are my art
and whose silence became my voice.

and

Michael

Who taught me how to be a man.

and

Delphine

Tu corazon es un poema

ACKNOWLEDGMENTS

"Statistics" and "Well Meant" appear in *Poetry NZ. (New Zealand)*

"Thanksgiving," "Road Block," "Corned Beef" and "Mammy Wagons" appear in *Dazzling Mica: A Journal of Poetry & Culture (USA).*
"Stabet Mater" appears in *Solo #6.*

I owe so much to love; and the generosity of these people –

My family – Daphne, Michael (RIP), Mark, Charles, Greg, Stella, Nnenna, Simone, Philomena, Bruno and Delphine.

Teachers and friends – Moris (Musa) and Nina Farhi, Ron Gottesman and Beth Shube, Elaine Attias, Harold Pinter, Mai Ghoussoub, Andre Gaspard, Sarah Al-Hamad and everyone at Saqi Books, Carol Muske-Dukes, David St. John, Percival Everett, Pamela Macintosh, Jennifer Dobbs – your gift is more precious than you know, Kwame Dawes, Wendy Belcher, Elias and Elsa Wondimu, everyone at Heritage Book Shop, Miabiye George, Kubie George, Al Rowlands, Banji Olafisoye, Sasha Mosley, Titi Osu (how could I have missed you out in Kalakuta Republic?), Helena Igwebuike, Jillene Tipene – soul sister, Meri Nana-Ama Danquah, Amy Schroeder, Rick Reid, Bridget Hoida, Joy Harjo, Eloise Klein-Healy, Ola Onabule, Harold Klemp, Michael Owens, Tindor Saki, Felix Ugboma, Clayton Eshleman, Steve Isioardi and Jeannette Lindsay, Rita-Ann Higgins, Wole Soyinka, Linda Pollock, Jose Ramirez for a great cover, Shabbir Banoobhai, Keorapetse Kgositsile, Tim Jackson, Lucy Popescu, and Kate Gale and Mark E. Cull for believing in this book.

PEN USA West and The Prince Claus Fund of the Netherlands – thank you for the support and recognition.

All the independent bookshops – you keep poetry alive.

There are so many people I owe; if you are not listed here, you are more importantly, listed in my heart. Thank you.

TABLE OF CONTENTS

AUTHOR'S NOTE

One of these days, I will write a book that does not need an author's note!

This book has many ambitions, namely –

To subvert the epic while playing within the field of its tradition. So this epic is about a woman, and though set against a background of war, it subverts the mythic hero and centers love. The male narrator's voice self-consciously breaks in to point to its architecture and mythic process.

Thus also pointing to the eternal struggle between the hidden and the visible, and the sleight of hand required by the writer to mask architecture, while wrestling with the moment of revelation. When, how, what?

The backdrop of this book is the Nigerian-Biafran civil war. This war was fought in the late sixties and ended in the early seventies. It occurred six years into Nigeria's independence and like the later Rwandan tragedy, operated along ethnic lines. The Igbo's, after repeated pogroms against them, seceded and declared themselves an independent country. The rest of Nigeria, backed by Britain, the USA, the then USSR and Israel declared war on the fledging state that depended only on France for military support. Nigeria, under the leadership of General Gowon, employed starvation as its main weapon. Over one million children starved to death in the three years the war lasted.

But here, the war, by its very specificity, attempts to point to the universality of experience. This war could have happened in Vietnam, Korea, Rwanda or Afghanistan. It did, it will, again.

It attempts to explore what it is like, not for soldiers, but the true victims of war, civilians.

The book also attempts to play with the notions of memory and memoir. At some level, it is the story of my mother's life – poor woman, the violence I do to her here!

There is pain, sorrow and death here. But there is also much to give you courage.

Bright Moments

Chris Abani
Los Angeles, 2002.

Genuflection

Them hath he filled with wisdom of heart,
To work all manner of work, of the engraver,
And of the cunning workman, and of the embroiderer.

Exodus. 35.35

ONLY A SMALL PRAYER

I know nothing of truth
Towering like that first light,

unbending sacred river.
But my heart is unending

circling in a rosary that falls
heavy. Fruit from piety's tired hand

And there is the rumor –
This is love, this is love

But what do I know of its lonely stations,
the full heft of a cross, the tenderness of rivets

But there is redemption in this enterprise –
Truth as memory's best guess.

So I rummage with grubby hands,
fashioning in stiff cardboard

and paste, her yesterdays,
like a project from Blue Peter or Sesame Street –

Claiming something caught in the shadows
between couplets overflowing with promise

inventing me, this child, this boy, this man
and my heart knows the stars I see,

knows others have traveled
this dark path before; to poetry.

Daphne's Lot

"The mistake they make, most of them,
is to attempt to determine and calculate,
with the finest instruments, the source
of the wound"

—Harold Pinter
A note on Shakespeare

1945

When the magic mushroom clouding Hiroshima cleared
on peace, Daphne was fourteen. Her imagination could

not measure the desert of death that was Normandy's
beach or the oily cough of tanks through small dusty

Italian towns where everybody wanted to be Americano!
But she remembered waking to the siren of the air-raid

alarm, disoriented by blacked out windows.
The shelter; a family huddle under the stairs

with the musty smell and the tang of cleaning products,
face pressed into the familiar hardness of the ironing board.

There was the thrill of the gasmask and the free candy
she got at the local cinema on Saturdays if she

remembered to bring it along, and the ballerina in her
music box that lived only when she hoarded sweets.

2001

I pretend to smoke my pen, listening to Beethoven's
Moonlight Sonata. This is the thing.

Long hours, late hours, much of it tortured
waiting for sense, like patterns in the sand

or language poetry or conceptual art.
To say: Oh Christ, my craft and the time it is taking

But Derek Walcott got there first and how
do you follow a poet like that?
I cannot call my mother. It is four a.m., this late,
the tone would be loud enough to touch.

I want to ask – did Granny brush your hair,
the moment fragile yet tensile as a strand of that hair?

I need the material, but this thing, this shape
cannot be found with her. Like the Rebbe said,

never give up a good question for an easy answer –
And this much – I know the deeper art

is to follow where the shape leads,
but my fear needs a map. Lines, in couplets,

to contain the uncertainty. Still it mocks me.
Oh Christ, my craft, and the time it is taking.

1937

There had not always been the war, unfettered
weed in the garden of Europe, over-running neat

boundaries, like the one Grampy tended and grew
the flower Mum would be named after.

There had not always been the austerity shrinking
joy to a half remembered child's song or unwilling

parlor games shadowed by boredom. Daphne remembers
village fetes with prize pumpkins, cakes, pies, needlepoint,

dancing displays, of which she was part, tombola stalls,
coconut shies, darts and sandwiches in untidy piles.

2001

There are memories we carry forgotten
only to stumble over them suddenly,

like the lost fingering of a B Blues scale;
Flooding visceral, and whole as the ball we bounced

off heat-wet tarmac, ghosts at the edge of night.
Daphne had forgotten she was the only girl to pass

the eleven plus exam in 1942, even as Hitler opened
up the Russian front. She turned down the scholarship

to Grammar school, choosing the Secretarial.
And though she tries, the regret is heavy in her voice,

Like the smell of mangoes
rotting − sweet, so sweet −

What was the fascination with the black metal
machines built by Remington that fired sixty words

per minute in the hands of a pro? The labor heavy
way the ink carved the page? The oily smell calling to a time

when scribes mixed lampblack
with bitumen and blood before crafting themselves

into myths old even then? Or perhaps it was
the impulse filling her diaries, defined in her evenings.

⌗

Henry John Hunt. There it was like the proper edges
of the desk he sat behind in the fading photograph,

pen held rakishly, the smile daring the camera to fill
the white page. Staining the yellowing back: *Dad. 1925.*

Grampy left school at twelve, though he loved
the classics and paintings – *The Blue Boy* in particular.

Apprenticed to a Bothy, his passion for color
transferred to flowers and shrubs. Daphne's

notes don't say why he left school so early
and why he chose gardening.

"Mum. It's me. About Grampy. Did you know why?"
Static depersonalizes the distance, yet I clearly hear

her sip hot tea before: "I don't know, Chris.
Those were different times. Is it important?"

My silence is the rolling of the phone
between moist palms like an udara seed.

"No mum" Finally. "I love you, Bye."
Rushed. My discomfort shuffling

the photos that will not lie,
and yet will not reveal my family to me.

1948

The funk of barley from the Horlicks plant,
the grey of this town not even Winter's rain could wash.

Escaping the mechanics of prediction, Daphne did not
hit the factory floor but became the youngest

secretary to the boss, though she shared the same
canteen as the workers in blue so old, they were

like a washed out sky. The bleakness of the room
broken by the tired sun floating in the grimy window.

Gladys, who worked the night shift saw the grey reflection
in Daphne's eyes. Wrestling with much reluctance,

the cigarette from her mouth, she said through smoke rings:
"Get out lass. While you still have your looks, and can."

1950 – 1953

How small town girls dare. This may not be a recipe.
Refuse the scholarship others will die for.

Work for the boss of the local factory.
Leave that lucrative position, off the factory floor.

Become an au pair to a South African couple
Move to Maidenhead. Shocking everyone;

Single girls do not leave home. Leave the South
Africans when the children grow. Move to Taunton.

More shock. Bristle like a sharp pencil behind
the polished oak reception desk of an hotel, a hotel –

Come home on weekends to a family that treats you
like a celebrity. Asking questions. Awe. More questions.

Until the television arrived. Then no more
questions. No more celebrity. Each return followed

by: Shush, not now honey, *Coronation Street* is on
the box. She hated that ghostly black and white tube.

Other things required for the dare. Drink. Dance.
Laugh. Leave Taunton and move to Oxford.

Find employment as a secretary during the day,
at night, party or go to the theatre club. And sit
opposite your future husband. But by all means
be oblivious. Do not notice him.

1954

In the sleepy cold academia of Oxford that had
more bicycles than China, she became his reason.

He found excuses to visit the College office –
Applications to the glee club that could not be trusted

to the postman. Essays for his postgraduate in Geography:
handed in early. She pretended not to see him.

Though the horns on her spectacle frames seemed perkier.
Finally, he asked. "I'd be delighted" she replied.

The cafe probably had a name like Joe's or Harry's –
an avant-garde cappuccino bar. In black and chrome,

it held the participatory promise of beatnik-Kerouac-
Jazz-poems-and always, the steam of coffee.

When they met on a winter's eve for that first date,
Mum felt, as she drank in the dark Coffee

of his skin, that she was turning. The mist on
her glasses softened him into the man she hoped for.

❊

Then the party later and the American rock and roll
that seemed made for the easy looseness of his waist;

eliciting envious glances from stiffer dancers,
whose practiced movements had been charted

across dorm-worn carpets, with the precision of calculus.
The subtle gyration of his hips as they danced, held out

the promise. Later he walked her home across
a gravel-crunching path hemmed by grass sequined

in dew and light. Was it his easy laugh, the way his
hand brushed her elbow – Present yet not too familiar?

It grew as she whispered to her friends at night;
warm as the hug of shoulder wrapped blankets.

✠

And what songs did they claim with the novel optimism,
and though Dad maintained their relationship was chaste,

Mum's shaded smile spoke deep. When did they cross
the imaginary line drawn by parents, and the convention
of society in the fragility of eggshells, whose crack
hatched passion sweatier than a jungle malaise.

✠

"Tell me everything."
Outside the rain was the landscape,

here in Devon, at the tearoom beside the sea.
On the table, the revolving tray, an island

on the ocean of white, was laden with sweet treasures.
His hands, like black gulls or the grumbling

of clouds before a storm, fluttered between the craft;
cups, saucers, sugar bowl and milk jug. Each teaspoon

an oar. He sighed. Reaching for a scone
he broke it open on his plate, divining crumbs

for the point of origin, buying time,
knife dipping, graceful as a heron fishing,

into the clotted cream before spreading the truth,
cemented with jam. The back of his throat burned

with the need of words not spoken, selected
with care from among the hot coals of his thinking

like slow roasting yams. There was the savannah
that rolled into a long ochre, dry pant. Trees

so alive they seemed to wear their leaves rudely.
Or the birds flaunting colors in the thick of green,

paws-paws so ripe their weight was a torture,
and yet the trees wept sap with each plucking –

The ululating song-call of women working,
or washing cassava roots in the river,

voices pulling your heart into your tears.
"I want to know your deepest secret."

Tea, gulped too fast, too hot, burnt past the crush
of words; Releasing: "My mother is mad."

Daphne's poised cup, the pause of her shock
came down with a clatter and spill. Then

her hand covered his gently. "And I am afraid."
Her silence, open, un-asking, like the gaze

of an newborn, was the thing that would
become her life with him.

⚜

Her parents had not met any black men until
Michael's purple-black sheen and easy smile;

Grampy said it reminded him of that other black
fella with the trumpet. And granny – little eth –

heating and reheating the spread 'cause
"They like hot food," until the tea was sharp enough

to cut and cucumber sandwiches
peeled away, like pages curled from use.

1957

Mum boarded the rickety propeller plane bound
for Enugu. Skeletal, like a sunburnt dragonfly,

it seemed held up more by hope than science.
Unsure what to pack, her cases, were swollen

from the uncertainty: Books. New sheets. Crockery.
Cutlery. Records. Slacks. Shorts. Blankets. Tea. Coffee.

Cheese in tins. A wedding dress. A little loose, in case.
Armed with only Dad's exaggerations about how

primitive it was. Bush everywhere and potentially hostile
natives, like a scene from a Cecille Demille movie.

She was pleasantly surprised to see Whites milling
everywhere, stores that sold Robertson's Marmalade

and vanilla ice-cream on crumbly biscuit cones.
Houses. Cars. Roads. No cannibals or wild animals.

And Dad, with his brother and cousin, their haircut
sporting a middle parting known locally as "I don't care,"

waiting next to a shiny new car that sat on
the tarmac's edge, its top humped like a polished

tortoise shell, curving away like a spyglass reflecting
all the possibilities around. The heat, like a fever

sweated out, forced from her pores, the illusions
about this land birthed in Europe's imagination.

And it was not a dark continent. If anything,
it was too bright for her new sunglasses, horn-

rimmed like her others. Was she disappointed?
After all, danger was half the adventure, half the romance.

And that first journey in-land, sticking to the plastic
seats. Did she take anything in? Or was she concentrating

too hard on being attentive to the endless welcoming
yammer of the men, while trying not to be sick

from the unevenness of the road, the heat and cloying
smell of melting hair pomades and petrol. Her stomach heaving

with every sway of the spring dashboard -mounted grip
of the statute of the Holy Virgin of Fatima. Like many

of the bad memories of Nigeria, she cannot remember.
But there would be challenges ahead, rougher perhaps

than the drive. She bore them all with a stoic resignation
that would have made any missionary proud.

The village was closer to the frame of her imagined
picture. No electricity; mud huts and sand flies

that feasted on her fresh, plump, pink flesh.
She lived in Ogbeka's house, roofed in shiny corrugated

iron for her arrival, and chaperoned until the wedding
in the local Catholic church; after her conversion

from the Church of England. The ride from the church
in the borrowed Land Rover, though bumpy,

was not long enough. Settling in quickly, endearing herself
on her first morning by frying plantains and eggs

for Michael's breakfast over an open wood hearth.
Grand Uncle Idume Chukwu, priest, shaman, seer,

bone-setter, figure as mysterious in family folklore
as Mechilzadeck, studied her silently with a wry smile

as though his shaman spells had lured her here, to this land.
Her place in Afikpo's Hall of Fame was quickly cemented

when she had three sons, born in rapid succession,
confirming her husband's virility.

That and the smattering of the native language spoken
in a painful accent, clear that she, the white one, venerated,

was humble, was all these honest people needed.
Dad fought his mother's derision for Daphne -

Calling her the pale wraith, with skin cold and pink
and goosed like a pig's or plucked chicken. Her blue eyes,

shadowless like a vengeful spirit. Not a doctor or nun
like the other whites on Mission Hill. No car like Mr. Brown,

the district commissioner. Dances like an epileptic.
Cannot haggle in markets or tell how long to smoke

fish or meat or what leaf makes a good soup
and which a poison. With hair like *mami-wata*,

useless for farm work as the sun would burn her
to crisp, like overdone *suya* – her mother-in-law

ranted, listing Daphne's faults. And Dad smiled
indulgently, translating: She really likes you.

Says you have translucent eyes and hair like a goddess.
She thinks you are heaven sent. And Daphne's

smiles rotted her mother-in-law's guts, as
nothing she said about her seemed to cut.

What became of it? In what unremembered season
Did it begin to unravel like a wick left untrimmed,

stuttering its flame, hiccupping shadows?
Was there a time when the exploration and conquest

of her body's mystery, inhaled along with steamy sea
smells was a madness for him? The warmth

had receded into slow dying embers, left too long
unattended by passion, and we were witness to ashes.

By the time I was born, it had worn to a habit.
Flared to passion only by pain and then it was just fighting.

⌗

And for Michael? First graduate from his town,
whose father had been a houseboy to the Irish priests

who recognized Michael's promise with a scholarship
to the university of Cork. Then Oxford. Did the burden

of the town's hope weigh heavier than rain drenched
firewood that burnt with reluctant and rebellious smoke?

In a town so self-involved that marriage outside
was discouraged, what did they make of Daphne, really?

What pressures did he suffer silently until that silence
sat in his throat, a rough seed of resentment?

Did he feel he had to prove himself unchanged by it?
The strength of his intellect, bent, honed itself

to a cruel edge. Not sure how to be what he never was
he perverted the lie until it was a barren river bed gloating

at his own fear. Like Achebe's Okonkwo, his bravado undid
him, stitching a shroud too tight to do anything but unravel.

And did he ever explore his inner skin, safe like
an umbrella's shelter, or did he, like me, shy away,

believing as he was told, that touching the inner skin
of an umbrella causes it to leak, the rain overwhelming?

1962

In those early days she kept dairies recording
in cursive script: Dawn treading blueberry

and orange footprints across the sky. Night rolling
the sun into its pocket like a child's forgotten yo-yo.

Streams crossed by bridges of slippery tree trunks.
The kiln-like heat. The sun yawning shadows across

the sand, melting the distant river into thick sluggish
chocolate. Air plants clawing sheer rock, ephemeral

as the sculpting wind, held by tenacious hope.
The river, where black swans dipped their heads

in regal acceptance of the fishes' adoration.
Dust roads winding like terracotta slashes against

the greenery. The silence of pre-dawn settling
like a casual blanket draped against the cold.

The single vulture beaked tap in the yard
where the clash of metal buckets sounded like swords

drawn to honor, as women carved a space to breath.
Dried, ready to harvest rice swaying.

Stars at night struggling against the deeper
darkness like fire-flies defying street lights.

Then changing mood with the abruptness of a needle
scratching across vinyl, lines describing heat

rashing the skin between her legs red, burning
in the salty sting of sweat. Then the deeper secret.

Gathering like dark clouds preparing to break,
it brewed thick like tea with too much tannin,

good only for curing buffalo hide. Then the fists unleash
the storm, tattooing her body in bruises like marble cake.

The violence always there. Then skimmed over,
for the children's sake. But that did not negate

the lie of her heart. She still loved him.
Then pages returned to the crackle of termites boring

thatch, drying clothes yawning in a cat-stretch across the line.
Her diaries held it together until the weight was too much.

Maybe the Greeks have a point when they say:
Love is in a pile of shit, be careful you don't fall in.

1966

When the troubles began, my family lived in Igboagu,
where locals were gifted in decapitation with farm

implements; the quarrel always over land.
Whose. Yours. Mine. Theirs. Identity.

Loading springs of station wagon low,
my parents and older siblings fled to relative safety

of Afikpo. A fishing town on the way to nowhere.
Period. Dead end. No strategic importance

to federal troops, they reasoned. There, in their newly
constructed one-storey villa nestled between Mgbom

hills, optimistically named Rainbow Valley, they prepared
to wait out the war. Sweat it out like a bad fever

caught in the trapped heat of blankets and Vicks Vapor Rub.
Life, unhurried as ever, made its way through despite raids

from planes too high to target effectively. Like errant
eggs from a basket, or nest, the weight of bombs bent

the air into an arc as they fell on surrounding bush
and farmland. The tremors traveled through the earth

to nestle in the navel. And everyone face down felt
the incredible awe of it, composing prayers like

a deaf Beethoven scripting orchestral maneuvers
from the vibrations. The salt-taste of tears, the body's

betrayal. Muffled sobs, ill disguised desire –
Like the itch of a match which is fire.

Finally the jets depart, peeling back sky, heat searing
it closed again. Standing, voices called melody first.

Then words. Spontaneous. Yet approximating ritual,
so we are not washed away by the deeper meaning.

Watching on the sidelines of the astral plane, and deciding
this was too much fun to miss, I pushed bloodily

into the war, screams on lips in December, clipping
Christmas by two days, a slight miscalculation.

My labor was Mum's longest, her hardest. Doctors said
my big head almost killed her. Shamanic grand Uncle

says I will need it for my life's work. Head butting
the competition? Mother says it was a natural omen

of an inflated ego to come. One writers need
to define, re-define, limit, expand, create, challenge

in the face of deity. Annoyed that my sleep was disturbed
by noisy bombs, I cried endlessly until Mum, pregnant

with Stella, stooped for me or asked my eldest brother,
Mark, to carry me. Face worn into a frown from my weight,

his ten year old muscles strained against the harbinger
of my current three hundred pounds. Later in Lisbon

he lugged me around till tears of tiredness, pulled
by the burden of this responsibility biting into childish

shoulders, ran freely. But no good griot gets ahead.
The tale has rules. Hard. Fast. Structured. Beginning,

middle, end. But like Jazz, room always for the gifted
to improvise, create, digress, circumbobulate.

2001

The Biafran flag's half risen sun was like a mind
not quite made up. Fluttering from a bamboo

mast roped to the side of a balcony, it is the sail
of our hope. Rays bleeding out, eleven of them,

spines that would curve into questions: Who are we?
What, tomorrow? Unlike the twelve tribes of Israel,

an uneven sum of our refusal to conform,
the eleven were meant to represent the still

unnamed provinces of Biafra. Or so the book
said. Maybe they were: The eleven principles behind

the new nation. Or the eleven reasons we were
fighting for our survival. After the exhibition

in the Tate Modern, in London, I hoped
the eleven rays had been fingers pointing to peace,

like the eleven stones which Michio Horikawa
sent to the world leaders in nineteen sixty-nine.

1968

When high flying bombers came round, again, Dad
decided it best we spent the day at Mission Hill,

Edda, with Father Frayne. Packing enough food
for the day, we waited while he went to evacuate

the Red Cross Station, its bright red flag, a clear target.
Mum also packed important papers, photographs,

what memories we could take, irreplaceable
or too precious to lose. Promising to return in fifteen,

Dad left. Even as his Peugeot cut a smoky path,
federal troops landed on the beachhead at Ndibe,

three miles away. The stranglehold had begun.
Hilary, dad's cousin, just back from America

was fly fishing, his hook teasing currents, flirting
with fish, seeking a bigger prize, a certainty

not possible in that snake of muddy-gold sloughing
old skin every second, never the same river

twice. He saw the heavy booted assembly;
cutting through back roads, he arrived

breathless. "We have to leave now," he panted.
Mum was adamant in waiting for Dad.

"Well I am taking my brothers," he retorted,
herding the older boys. As they left, Mark grabbed

a bag of food and Greg, Charles the storm lantern
that would prove so valuable. Seeing her children

trudge up Mgbom Hill and knowing she could
not be separated, Mum, eight months pregnant,

strapped me on her back, scooped up her memories
and pursued. Two miles later, Dad caught up

and we rode in comfort past long lines of refugees.
The asphalt, long dark river, winding down to hopelessness.

In Edda that night, high up, we watched as our town
was torched, the militia resistance routed

with a few crackled shots. The Biafran Army long gone.
Our warriors had learnt from the British that a cutlass

and a brave heart are short work for bullets.
Father Frayne, breathless from his gargantuan tummy,

helped us put up cots in Catholic school classrooms.
The integrity of the priest's house, bougainvillea

mortaring its brick, holding up walls, its purple stain
shocking the white wash, could not be compromised

by female presences, even in war.
Three days later, troops in soldier ant columns tracked

up the hill and we moved to Nguzu.
Those who stayed behind Father Fraynes and God,

were massacred in the Church, the priest forced to watch,
as helpless as his tears. In Nguzu, dad's friend,

a fellow member of parliament in the first
Republic, gave up his bedroom for us,

sleeping on mats with others. Hearing the gunfire
from nearby Edda and occasionally a scream,

I imagine Mum slept uneasy, waking often at the rustle
of death's robes, as geckos trapped our dreams on mud walls

that crumbled under their claws. In whispered prayers,
in the spaces between rosary beads, she seared God's heart,

bending fear to hope. Then. On the move
again, route carefully mapped by Dad.

We separated from granddad and other family.
There were no tears or hugs. Just tight hand shakes,

casual mind-how-you-go's and gruff grunts.
But it was all there, in the eyes. They circled back,

cautiously using old hunting and animal trails,
a skill long forgotten before this war.

We moved on – Edda – Nguzu – Emekuku – Mbaise –
the landscape changing as fast as our circumstances.

Sometimes as night stole through a haze of rain
we would stumble into a deserted village,

silence hanging over everything like
the echo of a scream. The only sign of life,

hens meditating under a tamarind tree.
Huts wearing beehives of thatch, walls cored where

bullets had stuck rude fingers into the mud.
From the car window, a field of corn rowed the plain.

All along the savannah, intermittent shrubs nailed
down the carpet of unruly grass. As we drove,

the clay of swamp roads cooked in the heat of day,
cracked into fine tendrils, mapping our progress,

unraveling our future on earth's palm.
And the trees lining our flight, heavy with shadows,

foreboding, like the insistence of a storm's dark
lashing, kept us from sleep's easy. And its absence,

rather than marking the passage, blurred instead
all of our tomorrows into one unsated sigh;

a sweet longing for release. Nights were hardest,
lampblack, the primal stain of nightmares.

Parked underneath some trees at the roadside,
the surrounding forest let out its breath in a solo

mosquito whine, the bark of wild dogs, the eerie laugh
of distant hyenas, or the rope saw of a big cat.

Night eyes adjusted, filtering dark into grey
shadows. In a tree above, a monkey coughed,

irritated by the harsh smoke of a cigarette sucked
on by a skinny stranger shivering to the left.

Vines wound around trees; leafy boughs wrapping
the moon up tightly. Then just as quickly, dawn ripped

night's fabric, stars falling as dew, and we would be off
again, past deserted sidewalks scratching themselves

with dry leaves. Through abandoned villages where mud
walls crumbling in the sun seemed caught in the moment

before a sneeze. A pot of half boiled rice curdled starch
on a dying hearth. A door stood open, an exclamation.

A bicycle lay in a heap, its back wheel still
spinning. A full length mirror, leaning outside a hut,

wearing an elaborate carved frame of cherubs,
was mottled where the quicksilver had eroded,

furring like fungi across a lake. There were markets
where baskets spilt their contents self consciously

in the sand: a montage of plantains, oranges and melons.
The clenched fist-dome of the mosque, sieved by bullets,

lets in dust like salt to a shaker. The dead Imam clutched
a fistful of prayer beads, some still pinched between

forefinger and thumb where he must have worried them,
the wood re-grained in sweat. Once Greg thought

he saw ghost soldiers walking among corpses, eyes
cast down, backs bent by the weight of rain and sorrow.

Sometimes we had to leave the road, driving across grass
plains extending like a crinkly sun-burnt blanket

or the crust of a cold Shepherd's Pie.
Tall Iroko and silk cotton trees scratched

the sky at regular intervals, some wearing a yuletide
spirit in their green leaves and the snow of their white

feathery boles, hanging from top branches like cotton
torn from clouds. Others, nude, gnarled in silvery dance,

dared our imagination. Paw paw trees signed
the fading sun with five fingered leaves. The sun,

in response, flared a few times, then bled to night
on the knife edge of the horizon. Despite

the ever present death, hunger and gunfire,
the African landscape continued to unfold.

Mornings with the honest fresh smell of dew damp
earth, that like innocence in the heat of lust, was lost

in the afternoon. Lightening sliced the plumpness
of the hot sky heavy with moisture. Thrown

by invisible warriors, rain speared the earth,
each point bleeding mud. Death cloaked

by the heat devils puddling the black tarmac.
There were cravings for things we had never had,

dredged up by the subconscious from magazines
and TV, tormenting with the impossibility of it all.

Perhaps the greater craving was for life, sweeter
even than the cold vanilla of Boabab fruits.

⁂

Years after the war, Mum discovered Sister Twomey,
her obstetrician had confided in dad, that after my birth

and its complications, she would not survive childbirth
outside of a properly equipped hospital.

His original plan had been to have Catholic missionaries
shelter us if the town fell in his absence. To quarter

us with the Sisters of Mercy. We never kept that pact.
Later we heard troops ransacked Mission Hill

looking for hidden Biafrans, holding frightened nuns
at gun point while discussing the appropriate actions

to take. Finally as a deterrent, they shot Sister Carmalita.
Dad's route took us within thirty miles of a hospital

at any time. Moving ahead of invading troops,
we finally arrived at Mbaise.

To get to there we drove through besieged Owerri,
a circuitous route intended to avoid capture

by federal troops hovering like dragonflies skirting
the edge of a pool. In the bombed skeleton

of the cathedral, its dome an open O!
puzzling the sky, steel girders raking

the ephemerality of clouds, somber
novenas for peace were said by a priest

and a congregation rapidly losing faith
in the grand design. In the debris strewn courtyard,

the wind, tracing rapidly replaced patterns,
demanded oracular truth from the indifferent dust.

In that refugee camp in Mbaise, missionaries
catered for the strays of war. One stood out in the post

war tales. Grief plaited carefully into cornrows
that tidied jet black hair into an order missing from her life.

So young at seven, yet her sorrow was deeper
and blacker than the dry well where her mother was shot,

scraping for water. The other kids teased her
constantly. But she never spoke, or fought back.

When asked why, she said:
Dead people have nothing to say.

A few miles away, Emekuku held the only
hospital still working. Dad left Mum at least two

gallons of petrol hidden under fragrant ahunji,
the smell disguised. If he could not be there

for Stella's birth, he wanted to be sure
she could buy a ride to the hospital.

※

Mum's water broke and joined the invisible salt–stain
of other births a little over a month

after we fled Afikpo. Emekuku was still
relatively untouched by the war, but Stella

screamed into the world already fighting for her life.
The staff wanted Mum to stay overnight,

but she insisted on getting back to her other
children in the refugee camp before something happened.

Though only a breath away, the staff at Emekuku
believed the accounts of war were exaggerated

and when it entered the town months later,
under heavy artillery fire,

the hospital had no evacuation plan.
The death toll was heavy.

It is true what they say,
miracles find you in humble places.

※

Captured when Enugu fell, Father Desmond's arms
were broken wings, like an angel of the first fall.

They healed crookedly. Mildly put like: 'the tea
has run out,' he says "I was tortured."

Dressed in a white soutan, he explained his mission.
There is only one God, and Allah is his name.

"Mercenary!"The Hausa officer accused,
not confused by Desmond's Dublin accent.

Missionary. Mercenary. All the same
if you helped Biafrans. Taken back to Lagos

over many days, interrogations, beatings,
he was released with orders to leave Nigeria, posthaste.

As the order omitted Biafra, Desmond
tried to slip back behind advancing troops.

He was rearrested and given a one way
trip to Dublin. Weeks later, healed reasonably,

Desmond pulled all strings, bent double under the limbo
line. He was not alone in this. Many returned.

"It is the children you see."
By way of explanation.

�֎

Night, along with whine of mosquitoes, brought safety
from Nigerian bombers whose Egyptian pilots

would not fly in the dark. Someone's opaque logic
hired pilots from a nation who lost a war in six days,

but here we grasp at straws. The deal is always,
take it or leave it. Yet even in day's bright glare,

refugees haunt road fringes, shaded by palm trees,
too tired to run from these gifted pilots

who come in too high to avoid anti-aircraft fire.
These attacks are a respite from the daily trudge

up and down roads, dodging the enemy
in a chess game that shuffles ever forward

and backward, territories as ephemeral
as the hope of surviving intact.

☩

State House, the grandiloquent title was too heavy
for the miserly tin-shed that was Uli airstrip's

waiting room, Biafra's brave face on it. Customs
and immigration formalities pretend this besieged

fledgling into being even as it shrinks from the size
of Ireland to a postage stamp eighty miles across.

At night the generator thumps lights, when there is diesel.
Otherwise the runway lights, oil lanterns, flicker in the rain

but never extinguish totally. Even God is not that cruel.
Flights, irregular as constipated priests who on first arrival

ate only bread, not trusting the unfamiliarity
of yams, are held up by torrential rains,

or over excited anti-aircraft fire driven by bored troops
taking out flocks of night birds for bets.

The Holy Ghost fathers run this widened highway
sometimes called "The Sidewalk" or more intimately,

Annabelle, by pilots who swear she seduces.
Thinking of it as nectar nestling between the fringe

of trees; female. Occasionally a tepid crate of beer
comes through and the Holy Ghost fathers

drink till they break into Irish sea shanties
that would make a stevedore blush.

Pilots, passports stamped with the old capital's legend,
jibe Biafran officers about being lost,

as Annabelle is one hundred miles west.
The Joke, funnier because of the Igbo

officers humorless looks, all spit and polish
in torn, much patched uniforms stiff with starch of sweat

and Wellington boots polished to a sheen with palm-oil,
their gleam marred by tiny insects attracted

to the sweet oil. Sticking, they bubbled the rubber
into a rash. The war flies in the face of it,

belying every odd, held up by
a ragtag army and drunken priests.

⌗

We waited in Uli, nearest village to Annabelle,
the widened highway, Biafra's last working airstrip,

for three nights for a plane headed back to Europe.
As day's embers died into night, we would leave

the untidy spread of the town, houses scattered
like broken pottery, roads running like spilt water,

for the airstrip. The soldiers guarding the gate were gaunt,
their eyes reflecting the hopelessness of it.

War is a self perpetuating state.
After a while it is about nothing but its own sake.

In the corner, in the shadows, another
family crouched silently, wearing the darkness

like a skin. Night after, gathered in the little,
hot zinc shack serving as an Airport lounge,

we counted moths slamming to death on the thick
glass of paraffin lanterns. Games Mum played

to distract us from the sounds of encroaching gunfire
and the boredom of the wait. Patiently we watched

planes come and go followed by Mark and Charles'
questions. Why not that one Mum? I imagine she

smiled resignedly in face of constant pestering.
We cannot take a plane that stops overnight

at Sao Tome. Because they don't let Biafrans
stay overnight, sweetie. Because the Portuguese

government won't let us. Because the Nigerians
will bomb it. Aren't we Nigerians? We used to be,

but now we are Biafrans. Hush now!
Sometimes we sat outside; it was cooler around

the fire that twitched sparks into the dark. We waited,
reunited with Father Frayne, our breath caught

in a choke as we heard big guns approach.
Finally a plane limped in, slicing a gash

in the jungle. It would leave in an hour
and we could go on one condition.

We had to fly on the outbound plane from Sao Tome,
which had a burst tyre with a temporary patch.

It was a risk less frightening than the encroaching
gunfire. The question hung in the air pregnant.

Father Frayne nodded. Mum, confident of the priest's
power, consented. We landed in Sao Tome, island

off the coast of Gabon, in time for breakfast.
Our stomachs, fisted in hunger, could not cope

with fried bacon, eggs, sausage. So French
mercenaries offered chocolate and smiles

as the Lisbon plane refueled. Mum was extra edgy
as we touched their guns. Hours before in Uli,

she almost lost Mark and Charles to Biafran guns.
My memory, cut and framed from stories,

(no doubt fueled by romance) is as follows:
the Catholic Relief Agency plane unloaded food,

clothes, medicines and Bibles. We began to board,
escorted by the Portuguese crew, frail old

missionaries and desolate Catholic priests and nuns.
The infamous Boys Brigade, Biafra's child army,

stopped us for a final search, to steal what valuables
they could. Ranging eight to fifteen, they bristled

with old rusty rifles, Dane guns, cutlasses and clubs.
Expert fingers sorted, divorcing nuns from Christ by stealing

gold wedding bands, priests lost glasses, watches,
Biafran pounds, worthless but better than nothing.

Mum had only papers, her bag of memories, the clothes
we stood in, and us. In disgust, they reached for Mark.

At ten, they argued he could fight. To prove their point
they threw a rifle at him. Reflex, he caught it.

"See? Expert soldier," the insolent teenage commander said.
Mum pulled herself up, staring down his rifle barrel

and declared in loud voice "I am taking him. He is
my son." Her voice did not shake, blue eyes flinty.

My mother, who panics when a teacup is broken
from a matching set, staring down death. Finally

the pimply faced commander conceded. But Mark
only gave up the heft of the rifle with a fight,

pulled by some invisible connection to these child
warriors. Mum insists differently. I prefer my version.

The dying sun spread a purple wine stain across
the evening sky as afternoon fluttered and died.

Just before we left, everything was still.
Then as night gathered its skirt, we took off,

cabin lights dimmed, treetops rustling fuselage,
as we flew low, avoiding radar. The captain warned

us we would fly in darkness over Nigerian waters,
reassuring us any turbulence was "only anti-aircraft fire."

Through dark windows, fireworks, tennis balls
of phosphorescence exploded, too beautiful

to be tracers from the guns below. Mum and Father Frayne
got the only two seats, the rest of us huddled on the floor.

Cargo planes have few seats or safety belts,
no stewardesses with sickly smiles to stanch fears of crashing,

belie the fact no one believes several tons
of metal will fly except by deux ex machina.

I remember thinking that if we were hit,
we would be devoured by the sea circling sharks wearing

a lace of multicolored jelly fish. But I could not have.
I was 18 months old. We reached Lisbon twelve hours

later with no further incident except when
Charles, teeth locked in terror around the rim of glass

of water, took a bite and swallowed.
The piece of glass was never found.

1968

Standing next to a breathless Frayne, his stomach
the envy of any Sumo, we realized the Church

sent no-one to meet us at Lisbon airport;
busy, foreign. Frayne commandeered a taxi

to the nearest convent, where the nuns sniffingly
paid the fare. Leaving after a hearty lunch,

he caught a plane onto London. From Heathrow
he called Gran before flying on to Liverpool.

We had to wait; six seats on standby at peak
of tourist season is a bit of a stretch.

Arrangements hurriedly made meant we had to spend
the night in the convent, leaving for a Catholic Lay

pension at dawn. There in that city of hope,
under the watchful eye of the pale, plaster Christ

on the Cross, arms held high by realistic rivets,
blood rusting down gaunt body, we ate dinner with the nuns.

High ceilings, bare stone floor (Mum recalls mosaic),
and austere furnishings, wrapped us in a hush

penetrated only by nostril-tickling incense,
the solemn reading of scripture, rustling garments

discreetly adjusted, masked coughs, the warm bead-roll
of rosaries and the apology of cutlery.

It was no place for five noisy children and a tired mother,
but they coped. They spoke no English and we

did not understand their haughty elegant Portuguese.
French, badly spoken on both sides, filled the silence.

❖

At the Catholic pension, run by members of the lay
order, we found others ousted by Biafra's war.

All the expenses were paid by the convent.
Accompanied by the other refugees, we toured Lisbon,

with the convent's gift of two hundred dollars.
Lisbon, in silhouette is Portugal's nose.

The inlet for the River Tagus opens
into a lagoon spanned by the Ponte Salazar.

Modeled after the Golden Gate, it was built
in nineteen sixty-six, in anticipation of my visit no doubt.

Christ, 92 feet tall, arms spread in benediction,
guards the river from the South Bank every bit

as impressive as its proto, the Cristo Redentor
in Rio. Trams haul up steep hills.

Torre de Belem noses inquisitively
into the Tagus, the starting point of many

journeys of discovery, like a giant discarded boot,
its wearer crossing the Atlantic to fall off

the edge of the world. Adorned with rope
carved from stone, open balconies, shield-shaped battlements

and Moorish style towers, it floats like a ship
riding the waves of Portugal's faith.

Like curious cranes, cannons peep out of gun ports, mouths open
in pant, in the vaulted dungeon, pretending the airs

of a Cathedral. Inside the Esufa Fria, gardens
of the Parque Eduardo VII, a nymph hanging

from a mushroomed stump of fountain flirted with us,
her stomach full, rotund buttocks perched on

a disgruntled fish. In the Jardim Agricola Tropical,
the city sweated its exotic past in the gardens.

High pillars like ornately carved ivory tusks held
up the domed ceiling in the nave of Santa Maria de Belem

in the Jeronimos monastery, built in the Manueline style
by Joa de Castillo. Museums overflowed with bounty

from former colonies – China, India, Japan, South Africa.
Even an ivory salt cellar adorned with Portuguese

knights, a sixteenth century gift from Africa's Benin
empire. Our pension was in the poorer quarter

of Alfama, where cobbled streets cut narrow ravines
between crumbling stone buildings. Snaking alleys held cafes,

street performers, many of whom were from exotic places,
echoing the diversity of the past. Vendors of scabbard fish.

Eel-like, they were stacked like silver high tension cables.
The walls of our room, adorned with tiles,

charted Portugal's past glories in faded blue.
We stood on the restored battlements of Castelo

Sao Jorge and squinted in the sun, searching
for our pension. Below us, flowers, shrubs and lawns

mapped the public gardens like the abstract designs
of Islamic-Moorish tiles that dared hint at Allah's

form in the complexity of floral and geometric
patterns spiraling and twirling into formlessness.

A stone woman, shrouded from head to toe, prayed
by the tomb of Carlos I. The concrete fall of her

garments, so real I believed I heard her sobbing.
A fishing net of cable-car power lines threw itself

at the facade of the Se, the city's cathedral.
The Tagus swept up steps wide as an amphitheater

held up by two stone pillars like sacrificial posts
for the Kraken, up to the palace square,

into Praca de Comercio. Mark kept the postcard
of Eca de Queiros' statue, the great novelist,

inspired by a near naked muse whose lush breasts
haunted many adolescent wet dreams. Years later

I stole it and hoarded it with other treasures
like the soap that held my first pubic hair.

The vaulted arcades of the cloisters
of Mosterio des Jeronimos threw cool shadows

where we ate our picnic lunch with Janet and Winston,
a Jamaican couple from the hotel, ex ex-pats

of Biafra. Mum tried to feed Stella from malnourished
breasts that held mostly air. Smiling wearily she

turned to Janet and said: "I am not a good cow am I?"
Like a child's Lego model, the Aquedento des

Aguas Livers, the aqueduct of the water of life
spanned the Alcantara valley northwest of the city.

The monument to the Discoveries, shaped like
a caravel, sailed the square. Marching up stone sides,

huge statues of Vasco Da Gama, Pedro Alvares Cabral,
Fernao Magalhas, poets, writers all led by Henry

the Navigator holding a model of a caravel.
Landbound, the only waters he navigated

were the shark infested oceans of finance, court
and church. It was he who bank-rolled all

the important expeditions. Spread like a collage-map
at its base, the huge stone compass donated

by South Africa, held discoveries from the past
while pointing to the future. This small, now poor country,

once colonized much of the world;
then lost it all.

Like spices thrown overboard ships drowning
in angry seas. In this city, founded by Odysseus returning

to Troy and named Ilisipona, there was so much
of us bound up in the stones, meeting, now,

on the cross of many intertwined destinies.
Passersby gawked at the white woman

in baggy faded maternity gown and flip flops.
One black child tied to her back, three in tow.

Mark, ragged, wore a scowl from the strain of me.
Charles and Greg followed, trying not to trip

over the umbrella. Faded flowers traced
the faint pattern which washed out nightly

as she laundered our only clothes. Hanging
on the balcony, they dried in warm sea breezes,

oozing the stink of war. Wrapped in cool clean
sheets, we watched stars seed the night.

Sunday. Lunch. Mum, in her only dress, sleeveless,
came down to eat. But the door was barred

by the thin-lipped proprietress, stern face
pulled back by her tight bun, her head shaking,

finger wagging every word –
"No bare arms in dining room on Sunday."

Stumped, and with nothing else to wear, Mum shrugged.
Tugged by her commitment to save the poor,

the dragon lent Mum a shawl. Taken all in stride,
stoically. After Biafra, this was all easy.

Six days, we tramped and trammed through Lisbon,
merry as any tourist, waiting for a flight with six seats.

When it finally arrived, I imagine Mum was reluctant
to face the uncertainty of London.

But the telegram sent to Gran sealed it.
Having nothing to pack, we left the hotel early

and waited in the airport, bored, listless but quiet.
Children soon learn that in war silence saves lives.

Keen eyes assessed us, computing simple arithmetic
and yet wrestling with her Englishness,

the woman in the airport on her way home
with her family after the summer on the Algarve,

finally strolled over: "Don't mean to be rude,
but you look like you are in some sort of trouble, luv."

Eyes scoped, sizing, filing. "I'm fine really. I just left Biafra."
Though Britain supported Nigeria officially,

the BBC still managed to convey the terror
and suffering of the Biafrans. Moved beyond words,

this stranger offered Mum her pram, stroller, clothes, toys,
anything, everything. Grateful, Mum refused,

sure that Gran would meet us with what we needed.
The woman insisted she would wait

with us at other end, until someone met us.
Mum thanked her, trembling

on the verge of tears because the horror
never overwhelms you. Only the random acts

of kindness. True to her word, she waited,
husband and restless children leashed in by dirty looks,

for us to come through British Immigration
and customs, fashionably late.

1968

"I am sorry but you cannot be admitted."
The man was young, maybe twenty, his nose turned up

At the sight of a white English woman with five
black children all dressed in rags. "But I am British . . ."

"But your passport has expired. You see?" he pointed
ever so condescendingly. We had an international travel

document from the Red Cross. Stained, creased
and much-folded. Pinching it between fingertips like a roach,

he sniffed, unwrapping it gingerly, "mmhming" as he read.
Folding it, fingers as delicate as an origami artist,

he handed it back with Mum's passport. His expression blank,
fish-eyed. "Ah well, but it is not a British passport is it?"

"But they let us into Portugal without any trouble."
"Yes Madam. But that was Portugal." Sniffing again.

"This is Britain." Trembling Mum exploded: "Why you . . ."
But he was unmoved even by this wild woman.

"The trouble is you are traveling from Biafra. Wrong side."
His supervisor, drawn by the scene and the shouts

of an impatient queue, hastened over. Glancing
quickly at our documents, and noting our sorry state,

he seemed appalled by the younger man's attitude.
We were ushered into England with deep apologies

and offers to our carry non-existent luggage.
We emerged to find Gran and a friend.

All around, practiced,
the English stared with averted eyes.

⚜

Refugees in a small rural English village always make
the town newspaper, especially when a local gal,

Daphne, returns with five nigger-babies from a war in Africa.
The thrill of gossip was confused by the compassion

for her suffering and "God knows those poor children
are innocent, still that is what you get when you

go off to live in the jungle like one of them."
But many came bearing gifts in response

to the article. Clothes, toys, books, food.
They delivered all day, wearing that embarrassed

smile of the English when caught in an act
of spontaneous kindness.

⚜

Milngavie, a suburb of Glasgow, was as cold
as Biafra was hot, and far from its troubles,

yet news of children and other innocents,
suffering had penetrated even here, carried

by Scottish ex-Biafran missionaries,
returned from it, but tormented that they could,

should, ought to do more. An old family friend
gave a talk to Church women's group in Milngavie,

having asked Mum if she could cite us
as an example of people dispossessed.

Moved, they sent Christmas gifts of jumpers, hats,
knitted themselves, no doubt before warm fires,

arthritic fingers aching. Mrs. Bentley continued to send gifts
until she died. This is all I know of this woman.

✳

We fed on steak and kidney pie, fish and chips,
crisps and Spam sandwiches, waiting out the war

in a sleepy English village suffused
with the summer drone of eager bees,

and the brambly tumble of ripe gooseberries
at the gardens end where fairies roosted in my

dreams, while Mum in her deck-chair read and reread
the very occasional letter from Dad

that filtered through the war. There, buried among
a catalogue of troop movements, the details

of casualties. Among descriptions of exaggerated
heroics and grotesque deaths, technical descriptions

of scientific advances made possible by the war.
Like cars powered by sugarcane fuel, homemade

land mines nicknamed Ojukwu kettles, medical
miracles, the invention of the cholera vaccine

by Professor Njokubi, an Igbo. Among propaganda
sound-bites: FREE BIAFRA, SUNRISE

ON A DREAM, OJUKWU WIN THE WAR,
is the line or two betraying his deep

yet embarrassed love. "I miss you.
Things are not the same without you."

1969

The rain, though soft, was persistent and Mum
wanted to get us home. Biafran bodies,

not fully acclimatized, were vulnerable
to colds. We were paused by a woman's call,

who wanted to apologize, she said, for teaching
her son to be a racist. Confused, but polite

Mum wondered how this concerned her.
"Oh. it's simple really" the woman assured.

Her son had told her they had a Biafran
in class, a boy called Greg. We do, he insisted

in the face of his mothers rebuttal.
The teacher said to be nice to him as his dad

is lost in the jungle. How can that be?
She had probed. Is he black? Pondering her son

replied, "I'm not sure. I'll check tomorrow."
Her confession however, changes nothing.

This was the England of Enoch Powell
and the threat of rivers of blood. All around,

each act reducing the impact of good people,
racists jeered at Mum as she pushed Stella

in a pram through the village, forcing her
off the pavement and into the road.

Chants of Nigger lover. Gollywog babies.
If you want a Nigger for a neighbour, vote Labour.

Were countered bravely by Mark's: Disembowel Enoch
Powell. But it was all around us.

Enoch Powell displaced Superman
as the popular hero in the playground,

where white children goose-stepped past the blacks.
And though on the news it said Slough and Burnham

endorsed Powell's position by a majority,
when no-one was looking, they pressed

lollipops into my hand, ruffling
my kinky hair while smiling sadly at Mum.

><

Mum told me about the war I was too young
to remember. Her stories, spells to banish any

lurking trauma souring, the soup of my subconscious.
Night licked the last of day from the sky,

like a black and white photo turned inside out.
Gleaming stars, like teeth, over salted the dark,

drawing out animals whose rustles were dreaded
more because we were blind.

Ogbeka, ear tuned carefully, sifted expertly,
silently. Then his machete sectioned

a startled python into choice cuts.
Mum had refused to eat snake but conceded

to fried snails, high in iron. "I hated
their taste like darkness. Thick, muddy."

⽊

Tea cooling with night, Daphne rested, feet up
at the end of a hard day's work, as the Beatles said.

A tentative moon watched through the frosted
window, leaning on a streetlight for balance.

She worked as a domestic to earn money
for us to go to museums and buy books.

Puffing tentatively on the spoon handle, she stirred.
"Your lot asleep?" Gran asks from the kitchen.

Daphne's Lot had become shorthand for us.
As though we were an albatross around her neck.

Like Lot's wife dissolving, the salt of tears
reached her lips. Upstairs, we slept.

1970

There are color photographs of Greg and I dressed
in cowboy outfits, guns drawn against Indians

neither wanted to play. Of us on holiday
in Eastbourne, in a caravan with every modern

convenience, racing go-carts and riding tandem
bikes or splashing in rock pools.

Stella's ruffled blue swimsuit contrasted
with her dark skin so she looked like an exotic fruit.

We ate rice and stew with chicken, waving away
annoying summer wasps from spilt lemonade.

Mum's promise of raspberry ripple
made the spicy food edible. Children in Biafra,

swollen from kwashiorkor, died crying
for a mouthful of the rice my careless foot

scattered. While mum worried about cavities
from toffees, in Biafra, shrapnel, bullets, knives, snakes

and the ever present hunger tormented mothers.
In Wales, we stayed in a farmhouse crowded

in with another family. Warm, from too many
people levered into a too small space, we kept

the terror at bay. Milked cows. Rode tractors.
Played farmer. Yet in a smudged black

and white photo, framed against a white wall
I breath easier. A loner even then.

1971

Hardly able to contain herself, Mum applied
to return as the uneasy peace settled

like stiff thatch seeking comfort. Paid for by the UN
Council for Refugees, our tickets arrived

in record time. Five, with no memory of this
other home, my trepidation wet the bed nightly.

All I knew of Africa was a medallion –
a giraffe crowding thatched huts and a palm tree –

that Mum wore on a gold chain. Gran and Mum's
late night whispers, overheard, fuelled my fear

of an unknown dad. But Mum's determination surged
ahead of the telegram with our arrival details.

�

Lagos airport. There were no flights inland, so we
waited in the stuffy, hot box of a lounge

with no seats, filled with tepid water or hot
Coca-Cola that left you thirsting more.

While Mum was interrogated for being a Baifran
sympathizer. They had her name on a list.

Photocopies of newspaper articles,
grainy black and whites of horn rimmed glasses -

wearing geek. A real threat to Nigeria's might.
Protests were countered by threats of deportation

without her children. Bills finally changed hands
to grant access and secure seats on a "full" plane,

which was half-empty when we boarded. At Enugu,
the capital of the defunct Biafran Republic,

soldiers with guns and scowls darkened the afternoon.
Once again, the Roman Church saved us

as Dad was not among the expectant crowd.
An Irish priest recognized Mum from before the war,

and insisted we ride with him to the Diocese
HQ at Abakaliki, at least for one night,

he argued, while they sent ahead to Afikpo
for Dad. Post war roads were unsafe and there was still

too much hunger holding too many guns
out there. Tired, resigned, Mum agreed, hiding

her disappointment under a film of dust.
After dinner, Father Casey distracted Stella and me

with magic tricks. Later Mum came to bed
and I dreamt her tears fell tenderly over me

like the gossamer gauze of a mosquito net.
She could sense that something was wrong.

Dad's absence shielding some terrible truth.
With no facts, she imagined the worst. Until dawn

brought light rainfall and Dad. Surprised, flustered,
torn, not expecting us. We bundled into his cranky,

hot Peugeot, for the long and silent drive
to the village, and I car-sick so frequently

Dad snapped: "This is Africa, toughen up!"
I never knew how, but Mum discovered

that the elaborate charade had been to protect her
from meeting Dad's war mistress and daughter.

But Rosemary, my half-sister,
would prove to be only one of many.

⁂

Daphne's diary spun a wish too precious to speak.
I want a man who smiles when he talks about me.

Smiles because he knows all of me and loves all
of me and does not want me to change any of me.

I want a man like that. A man whose voice
is the pressure on my hips when he calls

my name. Whose shallow breathing traces
the arousal of my nipples as I cook him dinner.

Whose laugh dips between my legs, catching
me by surprise and rocking. Whose hands

are rough when he touches my face honestly.
Whose embrace is desperate as though

I were the only thing keeping him from drowning.
Whose lips are moist with desire when he kisses me

and whose eyes dance with a dangerous fire.
I want, I want, I want a man like that.

※

2 by 6. The short column wears the tiara title,
Thank you from Nigeria, in the *Maidenhead*

Advertiser, December 10, nineteen seventy-one.
It states that Mrs. Bromley of the WRVS

received a letter from Dad, thanking her
and the organization for their help during

that difficult time. "May I express my sincere
appreciation and thanks for all the great help you gave

my family. They are now settled happily
in my village . . ." The extract reads. I used

to imagine Dad wrote it in artistic copperplate,
but it is not his style. No doubt his secretary

typed it, his only contribution the dictation
and signature, the flourish worthy of Picasso.

But it does not matter to Mrs. Bromley who said;
"This letter gave me as much pleasure as any I have

ever received." No doubt shared with gathered cronies
over biscuits and too milky weak tea.

※

Photographs never lie. Black and white. Time,
events, frozen. Souls straining to escape confines

of white borders. Our return to Amaizu, Afikpo.
It is all there, perfectly preserved in Mum's

red leatherette album with Greek deities
fading in gold trim. I do not remember it.

The welcome home ceremony. Makeshift palm-frond
shelters shielding sun and clouds, a field of wildebeest

grazing the sky. Mounds of food, drummers, dancers,
fading into kicked up dust. Fused in the shade

of our new mud bungalow, I lurked sulkily,
tickled by the sun filtering through holes

in the thatch. But I do remember that everyone
spoke of the war in the present tense.

Okoh, my ten year old cousin and I shared
a class, Elementary One. We sat under

a Gmelina tree, makeshift desk and chairs made
from cement blocks for our new classrooms,

dodging bird shit from bright yellow weavers
whose chattering almost drowned out the teacher.

A backfiring car had Okoh diving for cover,
his terror, shit splattering his khaki shorts.

The teacher laughed uncontrollably as we stared
in confusion. Frothing, Okoh picked up a stone

and did not stop hitting her until her face pulped
bloodily. Crying, I ran home and told. Later Okoh

was caught up a tree. Bound, he was whipped until
he bled, voice so cracked his screams were strangled hisses.

This was the war. Grandfather told me, even
the vultures fled at the depth of horror it brought.

He spat in the face of demons as he spoke,
because, he said, a land without vultures is barren;

the people cursed. Ghosts of horrors unseen,
unknown, pressed in as night spilt oily ink, palpable.

Burrowing deep under blankets, my mornings
broke in cold dried sweat and pimply itching heat rashes.

Once, our football fell into a banana patch,
rolling into a helmet discarded by a dead

soldier. Ebere ran out wearing it, waving
a rusty rifle in one hand, the ball in the other,

and the slogan on the helmet screamed: SAVE ME
OH GOD. The war was all around us.

We stayed after school and played in the burnt out
shells of armored cars, careful not to startle sleeping

vipers. Or we collected shiny bullets
from the prairie where Okere, the gateman,

said a big battle had been fought. We ran,
our screams warning ghosts of our presence.

Silently they lifted off in the purity of white cattle
egrets, fluorescent beetles in beaks. The heavy chink

of bullets, weighting pockets, reassured.
Careful, after Dike lost all his fingers when

the bullets in his hand exploded in the heat,
cracking like oil-bean pods, scattering his fingers wide.

The prairie ended abruptly in an orchard
next to a stream where bamboo's drooped like mermaids

washing their hair. Whispered rumors of Hausas
burying an entire village there, forbid us to play,

the fruits taboo. Defiant, we stole oranges,
running squealing and laughing to the safety

of the Anglican chapel, confident no specter
could cross its threshold. There on rough wooden pews,

beneath ceilings sagging under the weight of bats,
we bit into the sweetness of stolen sin.

Gorged, we slept until the squeaking bats left the roof
in a cloud at dusk. In the afternoon heat too intense

for lizards to bask, when rocks dreamt of river beds,
and adults slept wisely, we approached the orchard.

Hanging from our favorite tree, twisting, at the end
of a bright blue lappa, was a body.

Our screams woke everyone, and parents lectured us
on Eden and forbidden fruit. The water-weight

of death falling through the body to swell the feet,
pulled the plumpness of the branch into a curve.

When the body was cut, the branch, with hardly
a sigh, unbent the arc, righting itself.

Dad, irate like an old testament prophet
damning some unfortunate Biblical king,

was angry that the man survived the war
by killing his own children, when the federal

soldiers pressed cold metal to his skull.
The stench of his shame was thick in the heat.

1972

For years my father's temper and his tales about being
a commando in the war were more threat than story.

They held me trapped in a crippling fear that allowed
no room for self exploration. Only the desperate

need for his approval. He wore warrior marks,
several livid scars. One in particular, on his hand,

whispered dare-devil bravery in its deep purple-black
smoothness. Ravenous for glory, haunted by legends

of our lineage's lore, dragon-slayers and headhunters
at every turn, he could not accept his role.

Red Cross official in charge of distributing food
and medicines, the task had been more formidable

and dangerous than fighting on the front lines
where the only responsibility was to one's self.

He further undertook the risky work of reuniting
lost children and parents. This required a dedication,

commitment and bravery equal to any marine.
But it was not enough. So he constructed vague

accounts of valor as Captain in the BOFF, Biafra's
own SEALS, reinforcing this by terrorizing his family

with threats, sometimes fists, vainglory unraveling
in night sweats. Though Mum told me he got the scars

in a drunken brawl with Ogbeka years before the war,
the fear remained until that afternoon, discovered

under a tree where I hid smoking a menthol cigarette,
nostrils burning from manhood, nicotine

and the suppurating mangoes littering its base.
His angry shouts were chased by his thrown fist.

It hung between us, a metaphor of his loss,
suspended in my firm grip, as he frothed and kicked;

Calm detached, I saw only the frustrated
anger of a toddler with a broken toy.

❈

Ogbeka was nicknamed years before the war.
Like Karate, his name meant empty-handed.

Back then he fixed bicycles, his skills as dubious
as the scavenged materials he used. He was partial

to chopping customers who withheld payment
with a sharp double edged machete. And when the police

asked for the weapon, his standard answer —
I was empty-handed. Stout arms and legs held

up by a pot belly that belied the strength of fingers
like bear traps. Eyes, bloodshot from drink,

when he grabbed us, his knuckle rubbing our heads
affectionately, felt like pineapples were scalping us.

I always asked. Did you fight in the war? No.
He replied. My warrior years were past. But

he told Stella and me that he had helped Biafra's war
effort by killing Hausa soldiers on the sly. Why?

With a cruel glint he replied, "To eat them of course."
explaining what herbs soften tough Hausa meat.

His favorite part, the fingers, spiced, fried. We were
never sure if it was a joke, but it was our nightmare for years.

2001

The message on the machine is in my father's
voice: "Chris, this is Greg. The old man died

yesterday. Early a.m. Shit" I play it again and again
with fingers stubbing hands that look like his,

yet pretend a more gentle craft, pulled with the oar
of my pen. My tears, instantaneous, surprise me

as much as the thought that I would never be a man
he could respect; like he respected the honest

way Mark held his liquor or contained the world
in meaningful science, or Charles' competitive

edge and the way he held his own in fights.
Even Greg's challenge was preferable to this son

who believed in words and love and spirits.
The question is, how do you love a man who held

his over your head, just out of reach? And though
I am grown, I realize my heart yearns for him like a child.

To glove my hand safe in his, which is strong and hard
as the cricket bat I handled expertly, hitting my anger

in the red ball, yelling Howzaat! I call my sister.
Unbelieving, she says: "I don't even know why I am crying"

In response to questions about my voice, I reply
"No, I do not have the flu. I lost my father"

As though he was misplaced along with my keys
or the wallet my mum gave me when I became

a man at sixteen and which I promised never to lose,
but did shortly after. Let me count the ways in which

my father loved me: with fists drawing blood,
and real threats to rearrange my brain permanently

or to beat the monkeys out of me. With a meanness
that would make me a man or at least angry

enough to hate the world. He loved me in my
first book burning because he said – you should

be studying not writing. And when that book
won me, at sixteen, the second place in an important

national book award, he said: "If you were any good,
you would be first" In these ways my father loved me.

Yet I learned my inner shape in these ways too.
That honesty, at least outside of monogamy,

is the highest virtue and that my word is
my name and that is my emblem like an ornate

coat of arms pressed into the hot melt of wax,
sealing character. That success is good deferred.

He taught me the shame and embarrassment
of demonstrating my love, so that now when I say

nice things to friends, I fight tears of effort.
And here, in this book he intrudes in spite of my efforts

to keep him out. It would be easy with a key stroke
to erase him, but so much depends on the things

that cannot be replaced; like a red wheelbarrow,
or rain or white chickens and is at the heart of it.

And as I peruse photos of the funeral that my politics
barred me from, exiled from my grief, I realize

that I have never touched my father's face.
My fingers smudge the sheen of the photo;

his face collapsed in on itself. Skin desiccated
from the formaldehyde blooding his veins now.

Aunt Felicia tells me they could not get his shoes on,
as though all the water in him fell to his feet.

Not for the forgiveness that I begged of him
in that dream where he drove off in a yellow Volkswagen,

face turned away. Not for the ice-cream he bought
us as children, melted in with tiny red ants by the time

he got home, and which we had to wake and eat
in the flicker of lamps because we had no fridge.

Not for the words that I would have sold my
soul to hear him say: "I love you,"

did I return, or call, or write to say: "I love you."
The only time we hung out, on the veranda,

where we sat shelling peanuts and watching the sun set,
he said: "Find God for yourself, but make sure

that he is true, lusty, rude and alive." In that memory
I realize my deeper love – my muse is dead.

1973

Emeka, an older cousin, did not survive
the war, in spite of the effort of his mother's witchcraft.

He stares back from a photo with a cocky smile
as he leans on a motorcycle like a young, black

James Dean. His mother's magic employed a tortoise
shell stuffed with herbs and incantations, armor that hung

protectively over his heart making him bullet proof.
He did not die from the bullet that tore through it,

punching cleanly out of his back. It was the shards
of tortoise shell that shredded his heart like salad

cabbage. His mother still asks everyone:
Would you follow a dog to cat feces?

Before you can speak, she answers her own riddle:
You cannot hide the sun with your finger.

⁙

The "No victor, no vanquished" speech of Gowon's
at the war's end never washed with us Igbo's,

his promise of acceptance, sugar masking
vile malaria pills of our childhood. Depleted

by war, primed, ready to forgive if not forget,
resume our lives, rebuild, accept the political

construct: One Nigeria. Allowing no time
to grieve, heal, we reintegrated, playing down the cost

of human suffering in the interest of peace.
Our pain as translucent as a jellyfish trapped

in the sun bright shallows of a rock pool.
A bitter pill, but we scrunched up. Anything

was better than the humiliation of hunger
and a leader who abandoned us for a life

of luxury in a neighboring country, his name taboo.
Never spoken. All photographs burned. Become ghost.

Though co-conspirators in silence, we were not trusted.
Freed of corporeality, Ojukwu's specter haunted

Gowon, in the face of every Igbo. So we grew up
in the hard shadow of howitzers aimed at our homes

from military garrisons in every Igbo town, peopled
by federal soldiers on twenty-four hour alert to shoot

and destroy any whisper of rebellion still left,
flitting from baobab to baobab in silver moonlight.

Eight years they watched us while making our girls,
soldier's whores, shaming our men with beatings at regular

checkpoints, imposing random curfews, flexing their muscles.
Every morning, the call to prayer cracked the skin

of sleep. Sluggish, but then as the muezzin's voice ruffled
its feathers, the call rose to a single point.

As night shuttered down like the flower we call touch
and die, Mum read in the soft glow of storm lanterns:

They are changing the guards at Buckingham
Palace, Christopher Robin went down with Alice.

There were heroes too. Christopher Okigbo, torn
between art and the clamor of war, cried, Havoc!

and let slip his ravaged soul, profaning anger,
till Klepkany at the crossroads called home

the prodigal, to Mother Idoto. The surviving
handful of poems immortalize his genius,

grieving this griot cut dead. Others. Wole Soyinka.
Yoruba in a war of ethnicity, pleaded with Gowon,

at great risk, to end it. Starvation. Genocide.
This spelt death not only for the Igbo, he argued,

but for our collective humanity. Three years
in solitary confinement, *Shuttle in a Crypt*,

to silence his dissent. His trail was much publicized
by a starving press forbidden to report the war.

Life in Lagos went on as usual, far from
the maddening crowd. Wole is a symbol,

the possibility. But there are those, like my father,
who grudge his conscience; a publicity stunt.

Believing a man must never walk head bowed,
three years later, there was no sign of the hunger

and loss of war in Igboland. Self reliant, communal
effort rebuilt schools, homes, markets. Telephones

hummed harmony to electric pylons, army
of titans marching through jungle, and running

water coughed rust from dry pipes. Igbo's returned
to the North, repaired shops, lives, trade, uneasy

co-habitation, shamed friendships, fathers who
murdered sons for marrying *nyamiri*,

and daughters who tainted wombs with Igbo seed.
In once empty towns, people scurried like red ants

over a lump of sugar. Even the burnt out planes,
guarding the highway formerly known as Annabelle,

were gone, their metal re-crafted into utensils.
Forgotten. Vanished. Until next time. We too marked

the new. Dad's Peugeot 404, white, lines like
a fifties rocket with the sign painted on the back

bumper that warned: Left hand turning, no hand
signals. And our kerosene powered fridge

with its mirror for checking the flame that flirted
in blue and orange. And music. The Supremes

called *Baby, baby, where did our love go?*
James Brown screamed, *It's a Man's World* as Aretha

demanded *R-E-S-P-E-C-T.*
Highlife King Celestine Ukwu, the philosopher,

dispensed wisdom and dialectic materialism
to a heady beat. Then unexpected, but much publicized,

in September, Paul and Linda McCartney arrived
in Lagos to record *Band on the run* at EMI Nigeria.

The record never made it into the local charts despite
Gowon's threats to radio stations. But the photographs did,

in the *Daily Renaissance* and *Sunday Times*:
Paul and Linda like Jesus and Mary Magdalene,

wearing expressions of orgasmic-compassion,
arms outstretched in benediction to street urchins

who stared in confusion at the camera wondering
why these white people were touching them,

but their mouths were sealed by the precautionary
conspiracy of sticky toffees handed out earlier.

1975

At night, Greg and I snuck to Iyi Obasi, God's stream.
Lying on the wooden bridge we fished by moonlight,

smoking forbidden cigarettes as we watched the stars
gravel across the water's mirror. Occasionally a fish

would come up and swallow one. Further downstream,
in the swamp, where the river spilt mud over its bank

in an iodine stain, mangroves skated the water on elegant
fingers. In distant beer-parlors, arguments raged,

spilt with the licorice of palm-wine. Why did we lose?
We came so close. One hundred miles from Dodan Barracks

and Gowon. Ojukwu did a deal. Sold us out.
No, Nzeogwu. No, the cowardly Yorubas. No,

the Americans. They never helped us. And Lyndon Johnson
is quoted: "We cannot afford a Japan In Africa."

Always the barb lay elsewhere, for we are the great innocent.
My view? We ran out of steam. You can go only so far

on an empty stomach, empty breach, empty rhetoric.
It is all good. We are healing, picking gingerly

at scabs, their itch a fresh madness. All these years gone
yet under the surface wounds fester. The peace,

uneasy as a whale on tarmac. We negotiate thorny
issues, religious riots, flaring up a hatred, old, fetid,

lacking only the focus of a dedicated leader.
Nation only in geography. Demanding

equality, tipping the scales secretly.
To us equipoise is mine and a little of yours.

2001

I still have a bullet found as a child and carried
for luck, a warning worn smooth by worry. That bullet,

dimpling my trouser pocket is our only hope
for peace. Its heft is the measure of a yard too long.

Atonement for lives lost too young, the sacrifice
gone wrong. Optimistically we chance to arrive

there, the horizon of tomorrow. There
will always be quarrels, Biblical in proportion,

older than Eden, siblings fight. I cannot settle
that. I can only write a poem. But I know God

still speaks to us. His spirit, mischievous as a child,
employs the daily objects of our lives. Hair curling

a comb's teeth on a sink, reflecting the falling
that is our life. Esoteric patterns branded in tea

and coffee cups, washed clean by the bleach of our will.
No Elijah or old testament prophet; unlike my friend

Musa, I have not the beard for it. Nor that selfless
love of the world and others that grains itself

in the spread of our smiles. But the compass I found
meditating under a tree on that mountain

in Los Angeles is proof enough that I have
been blessed with the path through.

Cloisters

"The smell of blood already floats in the lavender –
mist of the afternoon"
—Christopher Okigbo
Come Thunder

WAR CORRESPONDENT

These eyes, framed in the aperture
fill you with nothing you can fight

or wrestle till you wake sweaty
and dazed, wet sheets wrapped mummy-like,

choking your self righteousness.
These eyes are empty:

The vacuum suck of quick sand, the dry
shovel of earth as you are buried alive,

or trapped in the hold of a sunken submarine
clawing your face as you slowly suffocate.

HELICOPTER GUNSHIP

Ujo – okwekwe nurum gba oso?
Okpa na huu, ka ewuwu mini na ma.

Nle enya n'elu –
Kpukpukpukpukpukpukpu

Ka okuku agwo loru umu ah,
Helicopter gunship na asuu.

N'chekwe nuru?
Oso! – mgba, mgbo machine gun

Na achum –
Tchutchutchutchutchutchutchu –

Ka nwa nnunu na ese ogugu
Beke di wonderful!

BREAK A LEG

His foot, torn off at the ankle,
Half wrapped in corrugated iron

Held the promise of a gift.
Jesus smiled sadly from the

Photo taped to his gun's stock.
Blood, like the rain, soaked everything.

The medic, impotent,
Suspicious, like God, lied.

AUTUMN IN BIAFRA

Autumn settles over Biafra,
Harmattan's red-dust sneeze,

specter of winter to come.
This season differs from Europe's

Hallmark card image. Dreaded,
it russets hair and eyes,

not leaves. Spoken softly
like the taboo of

a late night
whistle, *Kwashiorkor*,

fatal, swells bellies. Limbs,
skintight, split like sausages

in breakfast oil, marking
the fall to come.

† Kwashiorkor – a fatal protein deficiency that colors the hair and eyes red in its
advanced stages, swells stomachs and limbs, which split open.

THANKSGIVING

Even now nobody will go to the killing field,
near bald patch of red earth askew old grave yard,

where hate confused as duty, carved
the grave like a dog's open mouth pant

Lined up, rebel soldiers, every Biafran male
over twelve, crumpled and disappeared

behind the loamy horizon like ash
from heat curled paper; fisted.

Echoed by old Church to left, dense forest to right,
memory cracks the shots that linger in the heat.

Standing in the afternoon, eyes shaded by straw hat,
mouth sucking awkwardly on cigarette,

A Benson & Hedges, made in England,
he relives the moment he stood here,

One of twenty waiting to die –
the idea, not a bribe, was to offer, just before

bolts ratcheted home, ten rolls of Benson & Hedges,
made in England, to the officer in charge.

MR. WHITE

Quite the dandy, he wore white suits
Not caring he was a clear target for strafing.

Jets or snipers. Black shoes caught the sun
in celluloid flickers as he walked

Charlie Chaplin jerk as he ran.
Though he leapt for cover like everyone

else at the thunder of bombs or the pop-corn crackle
of small arms fire,he never stained his suit.

CORNED BEEF

Breathless, rat eyed, he watched the
khaki and camouflage ant convoy

tramp past his hungry gaze,
off-loading food into the refugee store.

Loosened from its packaging was
a tin of corned beef. He ran.

Fingers locked close to
His heart beating

meat, meat, meat.
The ants scattered in chase:

"Stop or I shoot!"
He did not, regardless.

They pursued his elusive, evasive
chicken run, crashing into walls, fences.

Arms pierced by thorns and grazed by
dry mud fueled already bubbling tempers.

Stop! The warning preceded by the shot
that slapped his back with chunk of

wall causing him to skitter to the left
and fall headlong into a near full latrine.

The war was full of small
victories like this.

WELL MEANT

Twenty-five hundred tins of tuna,
no can opener.

Powdered milk that loosened unfamiliar
stomachs speeding death.

Three thousand Bibles dropped into
Mujahudden children.

One thousand blankets and sweaters,
sent to tropical hot zone.

Crates of suturing thread and no needles.
Thousands of candles and no matches.

Tubes of toothpaste and no toothbrushes.
Boxes of high heeled shoes.

ROAD BLOCK

A blue Opel pulled up
in the shade of a tree.

A man is pistol whipped,
watched by toddlers suffocating

behind wound up windows.
To the left, his mother,

pounds on deflated breasts
begging for her son's life.

Outbreaks of cholera
in confined spaces cannot

be controlled.
Like Pilate, and though

he washes his hands eternally,
the order was his.

Two thousand on the first day
herded downstream where

the taut anger of the undercurrent
sucked them out.

Survivors managed shame with
the constant hunger.

ORDERS

These women fight on
less than a whisper:

The promised land is over the next crest,
beyond the next battle.

Unlike Moses, they dare not doubt
lest vengeful angels prevent entry,

killing them on the side of
hope's mountain

THE SECOND COMING

Dirty glass beads fall all
afternoon, caught in window's frame,

like the cheap draped off
back room of a bordello.

We have been told the end
will come like this.

A lazy rain washing
the air clean for the Lord

as the wind knits trees into
soft cushions for his feet.

Cloudy, the sky darkens;
Lightning as Jesus unzippers

heaven's wormhole.
But worry here is more mundane,

propelled not by God's wrath, but
an earth bolted Howitzer.

STATISTICS

International Red Cross' estimates
on daily death toll in Biafra is progressive.

In six months, July to December 1968,
the computations become,

legendary even for Nazi death camps.
3,000 die daily in July.

In December, 25,000.
Nearly all, children.

The Red Cross regrets this count cannot
include those dead unseen, deep in the bush.

3,000   6,000   8,000

          5,000   45

10,000   25,000

               12,000

10   2   20,000

13,000

               5   50

               1

REFUGEE

The man straps his coffin to a
rickety bike as he and his family fill it

with all their worldly possessions,
in respect for the way that is Igbo.

He pedals shakily uphill, his
family following behind on foot.

FAITH

Proof that an elastic band
returns faster than its outward stretch.

THREE P.M.

Jostling for space as the train approaches –
Hawkers: oranges, soft drinks cooled

by blocks of ice wearing loose jute sacking,
ground-nuts nested by bananas,

newspapers, neatly folded,
on trays carried by children.

Families: gathered to meet.
Porters: armed with wheel barrows.

Pickpockets: sieving the crowd.
But when the train stops

only the rain moves,
washing blood from corpses.

Even the strong citrus of scattered
orange peels cannot hold off the stench.

The train's mascot –
a woman with no eyes,

lashed down with hemp,
smiles in the freedom from lips.

From the gash of her stomach a
half term fetus reaches –

MAMMY WAGONS

With wooden bodies built over chassis and
cab, bearing legends in garish paint like

SLOW & STEADY or SINCERITY,
Their name derived from the local market

women who rode them,
their love as big as their

beautiful black bodies. These lorries
evacuate children and teenagers across the border

to Cameroon at night or move them from city
to city, ahead of death by a prayer.

ORANGE TREE

It is still there. Stunted, fruit hard, sour,
shriveled like old breasts,

the orange tree where he died,
hand vicing trunk in desperate hope.

That prisoner who escaped the nearby Biafran barracks,
his flight ending in grandmothers kitchen,

camouflaged behind baskets, pots, pans,
shallow grunts swallowed breathlessly.

Uncle fingered him, his smile cruel
as the uniforms dragged him kicking,

screaming to that tree where
they emptied bullet-hard hate into him.

Men. Familiar. From the village,
took the still twitching warm corpse into the near forest.

Dull thwacks of machetes shamed the afternoon.
Then the procession:

men, banana-leaf wrapped
packages on head, leaking blood.

STABAT MATER

Through gaps in trees, moonlight
veins night with the remembrance of

dawn. Among ferns stubbling the forest
floor a mother squats, watching the child in

her arms losing its grip on life,
its hacking breath, a suffering hanging on.

Gently she closes her eyes as her fingers
pincer its nose and mouth,

easing the passage across.
What detail can be true of the remembered life;

Place, event, lost like a flower's scent
stolen by a bee leaving only the itch of its sting.

MAIDEN'S DANCE

Women wear guns fiercer, their
hate more casual, stylish even.

Crushing the dream crushers who
freeze, stunned by screams

flung like medusa-snake braids.
And when the bullets finish,

through the silence; the intimate
suck of flesh romancing bayonet-steel,

the thuds of clubs, and
the grunts of effort satisfied.

WARRIORS

Grainy and faded like the mist
swallowing trees in the background

of a forest clearing somewhere in
Biafra, commando's, half dressed,

pose for the photograph.
The guns of those squatting in

front point to the optimistic smiles
of those behind.

To the left, a boy contemplates the
bleeding stump of his right arm.

PLANTING SEASON

The women we pass in the rice fields,
bent double with fatigue,

wear masks of ugly.
How else can you poke fingers into

decaying flesh buried just beneath the surface,
threading needles of green.

STRATEGIC TARGETS

Nigerian bombers drop a full pay load on
unsuspecting shoppers in Aba market at noon.

An act equivalent to setting off a bomb at
Grand Central Station, New York, at rush hour.

Those not vaporized or buried alive,
sun in the courtyard at the General Hospital:

heads, limbs and torsos that don't match up,
scattered pieces of a jigsaw puzzle too hard to solve.

FREE ENTERPRISE

In the bombed out shell of the market,
he sits in the shade of a hole riddled umbrella,

It is the day after and the market is desolate.
He dusts the hats and sunglasses

waiting for the break that must come;
If there is no food to buy, then perhaps.

PARABLE OF THE SOWER

Under a dawn drizzle, mother,
three children and father.

In his arms, smaller than a doll,
their dead girl.

Quickly dug, the hole is too shallow.
Kneeling, they plant her.

Benediction

"We can believe in miracles in this place"
—Kwame Dawes
ShadowPlay

PEOPLE LIKE US

Standing at dawn in Grandmother's kitchen,
hot tea mists the window as it warms me.

Outside, soft pre-dawn light drizzles over hens
scratching for truth beneath the stunted orange tree.

The mauve dawn yawns in the slow approaching heat,
exhaling dark shadows. As I sip, Grandmother, arthritic,

chops onions and tomatoes ready for the searing of hot oil.
Eggs crack like answers to unasked questions

and I realize, this is all there is.
The stitching of life into transfigurations.

BIOGRAPHICAL NOTE

Chris Abani has published two novels, *Masters of the Board* (Delta, 1985) which won the 1983 Delta Fiction Award, and *Sirocco* (Swan, 1987). His short fiction has been widely anthologized. He has written and produced two plays, *Room at the Top* (IBC, 1983) and *Song of a Broken Flute* (IMOSU, 1990). His last book of poetry, *Kalakuta Republic* (Saqi, 2001), received the 2001 PEN USA West Freedom-to-Write Award and the 2001 Prince Claus of Netherlands Award. The recipient of a 2003 Hellman/Hammer Grant, he is a Middleton Fellow at USC and teaches at Antioch University's MFA program in Los Angeles.

Printed in the USA
CPSIA information can be obtained
at www.ICGtesting.com
JSHW080003150824
68134JS00021B/2248

9 781888 996623